Creature Comparisons

Fish

Tracey Crawford

Heinemann Library
Chicago, Illinois

Photo research by Tracy Cummins, Heather Mauldin, and Ruth Blair
Designed by Jo Hinton-Malivoire
Printed and bound in China by South China Printing Company
10 09 08
10 9 8 7 6 5 4 3 2

Library of Congress Cataloging-in-Publication Data
Crawford, Tracey.
  Fish / Tracey Crawford.— 1st ed.
      p. cm. — (Creature comparisons)
  Includes bibliographical references and index.
  ISBN-13: 978-1-4034-8457-4 (hc) ISBN-10: 1-4034-8457-0 (hc)
  ISBN-13: 978-1-4034-8464-2 (pb) ISBN-10: 1-4034-8464-3 (pb)
  1. Fishes—Juvenile literature. I. Title. II. Series.
  QL617.2.C72 2007
  597—dc22
                                        2006007665

Acknowledgments
The author and publisher are grateful to the following for permission to reproduce copyright material: Corbis pp. **4** (monkey, Frank Lukasseck/zefa; bird, Arthur Morris), **6** (Stephen Frink), **7** (Jeffrey L. Rotman), **9** (Royalty Free), **10** (Martin Harvey), **11** (Kit Kittle), **12** (Anthony Bannister), **14** (Louie Psihoyos), **15** (Stephen Frink), **16** (Brandon D. Cole), **18**, **19** (Amos Nachoum), **21** (Hal Beral), **22** (shark, Denis Scott; flounder, Brandon D. Cole), **23** (goldfish, Martin Harvey; Indo-Pacific Bluetang, Jeffrey L. Rotman; gray angelfish, Royalty Free); Getty Images pp. **5**, **17** (Hunt), **20** (Westmorland); Marinethemes.com p. **22** (hand fish, Kelvin Aitkenn); Naturepl.com p. **13** (Doug Perrine); Carlton Ward p. **4** (snake, frog).

Cover photograph of a blue tang reproduced with permission of Getty Images/Mike Kelly and a white spotted pufferfish reproduced with permission of Getty Images/Steven Hunt. Back cover photograph of an Indo-Pacific bluetang reproduced with permission of Corbis/Jeffrey L. Rotman.

Every effort has been made to contact copyright holders of any material reproduced in this book.
Any omissions will be rectified in subsequent printings if notice is given to the publisher.

Contents

There are many types of animals.

Fish are one type of animal.

All fish live in water.

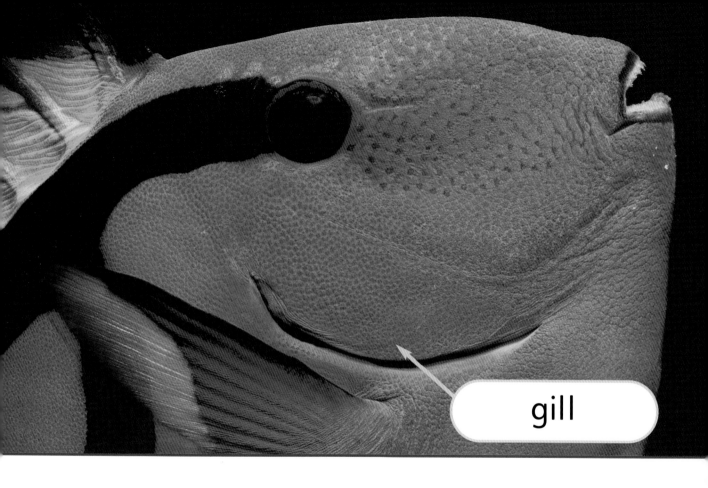

gill

All fish have gills.

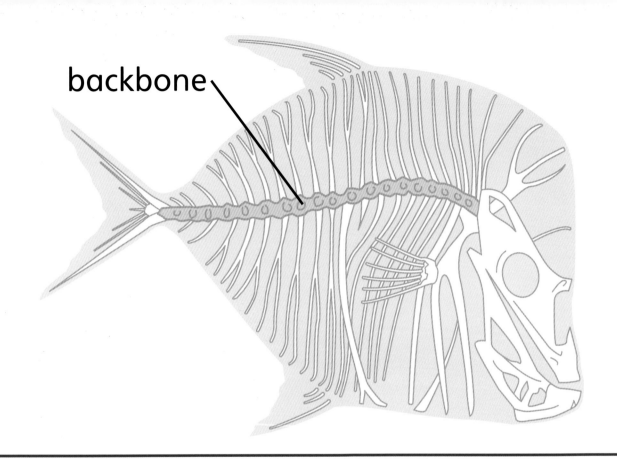

backbone

All fish have a backbone.

fin

tail

All fish have fins and a tail.

scales

Most fish have scales.

But this fish does not.

Most fish are born from an egg.

baby shark

But this fish is not.

Some fish are big.

Some fish are small.

Some fish are flat.

Some fish are round.

Some fish hunt.

Some fish hide.

Every fish is different.

Every fish is special.

Fish Facts

Sharks have many rows of teeth.

Flounders live on the ocean floor. They can change color. This helps them hide.

Hand fish have fins that are like hands. These fish walk on the ocean floor.

Picture Glossary

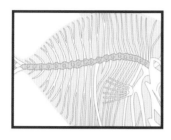 **backbone** the part of the skeleton that goes from the tail to the head

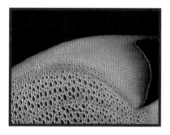 **fin** the part of a fish that helps it move through water

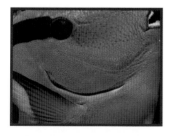 **gill** the part of a fish that helps it breathe

 **scale** a small, flat plate on the outside of an animal. Scales cover skin.

Index

Note to Parents and Teachers
In *Fish*, children are introduced to the diversity found within this animal group, as well as the characteristics that all fish share. The text has been carefully chosen with the advice of a literacy expert to enable beginning readers success while reading independently or with moderate support. Scientists were consulted to provide both interesting and accurate content.

By showing the importance of diversity within wildlife, *Fish* invites children to welcome diversity in their own lives. *Fish* ends by stating that every fish is a unique, special creature. Use this as a discussion point for how each person is also unique and special. You can support children's nonfiction literacy skills by helping them to use the table of contents, picture glossary, and index.

A Small Sheep in a Pear Tree

A Small Sheep in a Pear Tree

Adrianne Lobel

Harper & Row, Publishers
New York, Hagerstown, San Francisco, London

Library of Congress Cataloging in Publication Data
Lobel, Adrianne.
    A small sheep in a pear tree.

    SUMMARY: On each of the "Twelve Days of
Christmas," a young woman receives a different gift of sheep
from her true love.
    1. Christmas—Juvenile poetry.   [1. Christmas poetry]
I. Title.
PZ8.3.L8Sm3   [E]   76-58721
ISBN 0-06-023952-2
ISBN 0-06-023953-0 lib. bdg.

For Hollywood

The first day of Christmas
my true love sent to me

a small sheep in a pear tree.

The second day of Christmas
my true love sent to me

two turtle sheep,
and a small sheep in a pear tree.

The third day of Christmas
my true love sent to me

three French sheep,
two turtle sheep, and a small sheep in a pear tree.

The fourth day of Christmas
my true love sent to me

four calling sheep,
three French sheep, two turtle sheep,
and a small sheep in a pear tree.

The fifth day of Christmas
my true love sent to me

five golden sheep,
four calling sheep, three French sheep,
two turtle sheep, and a small sheep in a pear tree.

The sixth day of Christmas
my true love sent to me

six sheep a-laying,
five golden sheep, four calling sheep,
three French sheep, two turtle sheep,
and a small sheep in a pear tree.

The seventh day of Christmas
my true love sent to me

seven sheep a-swimming,
six sheep a-laying, five golden sheep,
four calling sheep, three French sheep,
two turtle sheep, and a small sheep in a pear tree.

18

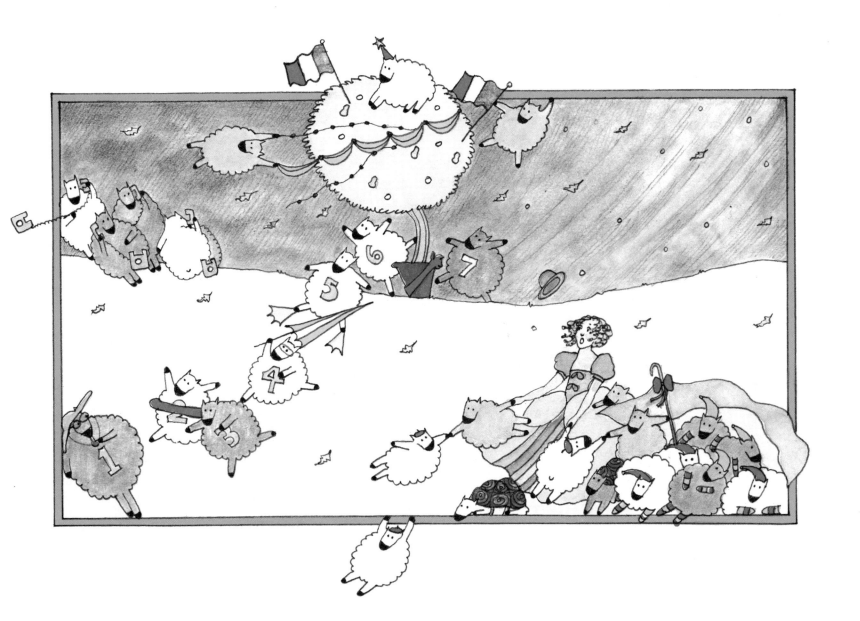

The eighth day of Christmas
my true love sent to me

eight sheep a-milking,
seven sheep a-swimming, six sheep a-laying,
five golden sheep, four calling sheep,
three French sheep, two turtle sheep,
and a small sheep in a pear tree.

The ninth day of Christmas
my true love sent to me

nine sheep drumming,
eight sheep a-milking, seven sheep a-swimming,
six sheep a-laying, five golden sheep,
four calling sheep, three French sheep,
two turtle sheep, and a small sheep in a pear tree.

The tenth day of Christmas
my true love sent to me

ten sheep piping,
nine sheep drumming, eight sheep a-milking,
seven sheep a-swimming, six sheep a-laying,
five golden sheep, four calling sheep,
three French sheep, two turtle sheep,
and a small sheep in a pear tree.

The eleventh day of Christmas
my true love sent to me

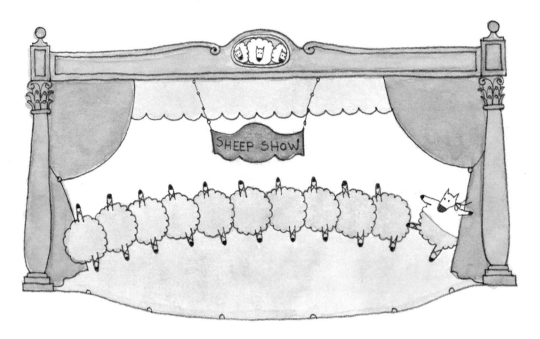

eleven sheep dancing,
ten sheep piping, nine sheep drumming,
eight sheep a-milking, seven sheep a-swimming,
six sheep a-laying, five golden sheep,
four calling sheep, three French sheep,
two turtle sheep, and a small sheep in a pear tree.

The twelfth day of Christmas
my true love sent to me

twelve sheep a-leaping,
eleven sheep dancing, ten sheep piping,
nine sheep drumming, eight sheep a-milking,
seven sheep a-swimming, six sheep a-laying,
five golden sheep, four calling sheep,
three French sheep, two turtle sheep,
and a small sheep in a pear tree.

Merry Christmas!